Sports Cars

Bruce LaFontaine

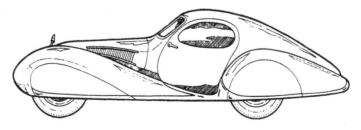

DOVER PUBLICATIONS, INC.
Mineola, New York

Bruce LaFontaine

Bruce LaFontaine is the illustrator and author of twenty-four non-fiction children's books. His published works are sold in bookstores throughout the United States, Canada, and the United Kingdom. Mr. LaFontaine specializes in history, science, transportation, and architectural subjects for the children's middle-reader market (ages 8–12). He lives and works in the Rochester, New York area.

Bibliographical Note

Sports Cars is a new work, first published by Dover Publications, Inc., in 1999.

International Standard Book Number

ISBN-13: 978-0-486-40802-6
ISBN-10: 0-486-40802-7

Manufactured in the United States by Courier Corporation
40802704   2013
www.doverpublications.com

INTRODUCTION

Experts and amateurs alike have tried to define the exact meaning of the term "sports car." But after one cuts through all the technical frills and overlay of opinion, these attempts may be reduced to the simple statement that a sports car is a vehicle designed to maximize the sheer pleasure of driving.

Sports cars evolved as a result of early automobile manufacturers' involvement in motor car racing, since a winning race car served as a powerful advertising tool to increase auto sales. The first sports cars were little more than modified and refined versions of the race cars of the era. As the market for these high-performance sporting automobiles expanded, they gradually grew into separate model lines offered by most major car makers.

This book gives an overview in words and pictures of some of the more popular and memorable sports cars created since the early years of the 20th century. The first sports cars were usually open two-seat "roadsters" or convertibles, although over the years, hard-top coupes and four-seat versions also became available. As the technology advanced, the sports car became faster and more comfortable, with precision steering and exceptional road adhesion capability. However, the defining characteristic of the sports car has remained the same throughout its evolution: i.e., an aerodynamic design that enhances the vehicle's ability to snake through curves and around corners in an unusually quick and nimble fashion. The thrills and excitement that result from such driving feats is the key ingredient to their success and popularity.

Since their early days, sports car engines have increased dramatically in size and power. The power of an engine is rated by its amount of horsepower (hp). Beginning with simple four-cylinder engines that developed less than 100 hp, they have grown steadily into engines with six, eight, ten, and even twelve cylinders that can produce over 400 hp. The size of an automobile engine is measured by the amount of volume taken up by its cylinder bores—the holes in the engine block that enclose the pistons. This measurement is given in cubic-inches for American vehicles and cubic-centimeters (cc's) for European cars.

Some of the terms employed in this book describe the various devices used to introduce fuel into the engine. The earliest of these engine parts is the carburetor. It metered a mixture of gasoline and air into the cylinders where it was ignited by a spark plug. Later devices were the supercharger and the turbocharger. These were used to force more of the fuel-air mixture into the engine at high pressure in order to increase speed and performance. Most of today's sports cars use the modern method of fuel-injection to control the fuel-air mix.

Performance figures for the sports cars described in this book are given in the amount of time required for the vehicle to go from a standing start (0 mph) to 60 mph, as well as their top speed attainable at maximum engine revolutions. Early sports cars had 0-60 mph times of 8 to 15 seconds, and top speeds in the 100 to 120 mph range. The current breed of super sports cars have astonishing 0-60 mph times of 4 to 5 seconds and top speeds approaching 200 mph. Throughout the past eighty-five years of their development, these high-performance automobiles have represented the most advanced and powerful vehicles produced in their respective times.

1915 STUTZ BEARCAT

In the early years of the 20th century, the automobile was used principally as a means of basic transport for people and cargo. But as they became more technologically sophisticated, cars were also utilized for recreational pursuits such as racing. The most successful race cars soon evolved into new versions modified specifically for sale to the general public. These models for street use were the first real "sports cars." One of the most famous of these early sporting vehicles was built by the Stutz Motor Car Company of New York City. It was named the "Bearcat" and it was first introduced in 1914.

The Stutz Bearcat was an open two-seater with a massive 390 cubic-inch four-cylinder engine that could produce 60 hp. This gave the 4,960-pound vehicle a top speed of 80 mph—exceedingly fast in that era. It's handling was nimble, but at the cost of a very bumpy ride. Both front and rear axles were suspended by heavy and stiff elliptical leaf springs.

The Bearcat's chief competition in the American sports car market in those early years was the Mercer "Raceabout." Both cars were very similar in features and appearance, and they constantly competed in races as well as vied for the motoring public's attention. To ridicule their arch rival, Mercer Motors developed the following bit of advertising verse: "You have to be nuts, to drive a Stutz!" Stutz countered with their own silly (and ungrammatical) slogan: "There's nothing worser, than a Mercer!" The two companies continued as rivals until the early 1930s, when the Great Depression drove them both out of business.

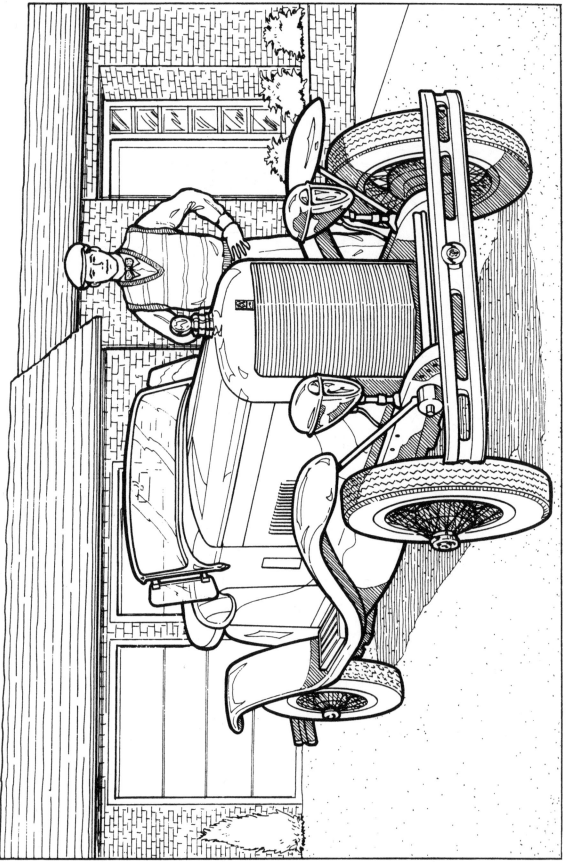

1929 DU PONT SPEEDSTER

The era of the 1920s was characterized by flamboyant Jazz Age music, free-spirited "flappers," and gangsters. It was also a period when numerous small automobile manufacturers sprang up to meet the American motoring public's increasing interest in these vehicles. One such company was du Pont Motors of Moore, Pennsylvania. Founded by E. Paul du Pont, it built a number of models between 1923 and 1932.

Shown above is a 1929 Model G "Speedster." It was powered by an eight-cylinder, "straight-eight" engine, so called because the engine cylinders were lined up one in front of the other. Other automobile engine types included designs with cylinders that were horizontally opposed in a box-like grouping, or arranged in a "V" formation. The number of cylinders could range from four to six to eight, ten, twelve, or even sixteen. The du Pont Speedster's 322 cubic-inch engine produced 140 hp and could propel the vehicle to a guaranteed top speed of 100 mph. Like many other auto builders of the 1920s, du Pont Motors was eventually forced out of business by the Great Depression.

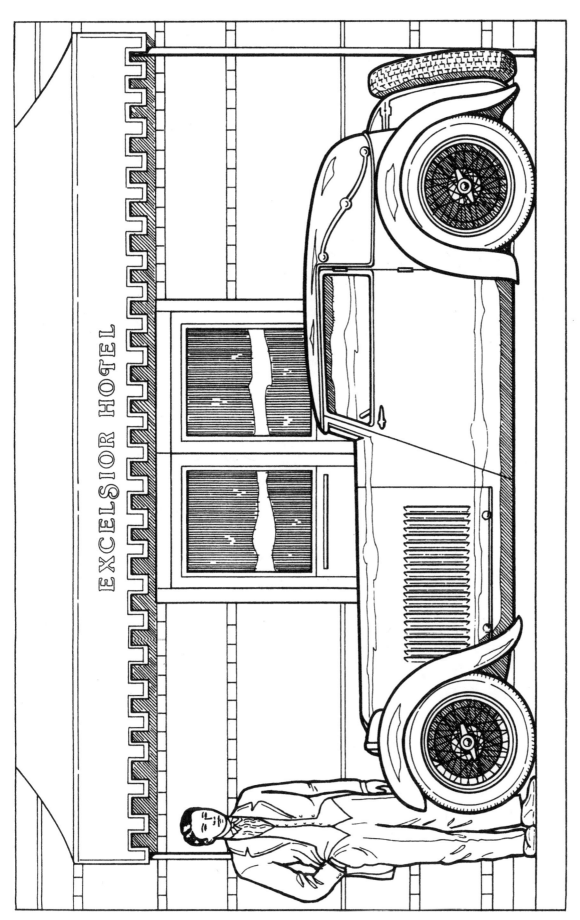

EXCELSIOR HOTEL

1931 JAGUAR S.S. 1

One of the most venerated names in sports car history began with the collaboration of William Lyons and William Walmsley in 1922. Their company was originally formed as "Swallow Sidecar and Coachbuilders" to make motorcycle sidecars and custom car bodies for other automobile companies. In 1931, they introduced the grandfather of the famous Jaguar line of sports cars, the S.S. 1 ("S.S." for "Swallow Sidecar"). This four-passenger coupe was long, low, and sleek. It was powered by a 2,552-cc straight-six engine that could propel the vehicle to 90 mph. Jaguar Motors would later build some of the classiest and most sought-after sports cars ever built, especially in the post-World War II years.

1934 ALFA ROMEO TYPE 8C ROADSTER

Highly esteemed in the sports car world is the Alfa Romeo Company of Milan, Italy, founded in 1909 by Alexandre Darracq, who in 1915 became partners with Nicola Romeo. In 1919, they formed the Alfa Romeo Motor Car Company which produced vehicles for the motor car racing market throughout Europe and the United States. Their sports cars were an offshoot of their line of winning racing cars.

Shown above is one of their most popular designs of the 1930s, the Type 8C roadster. Considered a classic example of Italian automotive styling of the era, this two-seat roadster was very fast and agile. The name "roadster" is a general term applied most often to open (convertible top) two-seat sports cars. The Type 8C was equipped with a 2,900-cc straight-eight engine developing 142 hp. The combination of this powerful engine in the lightweight roadster body gave the Type 8C a top speed of 110 mph. Over the decades, Alfa Romeo has continued to build highly coveted sports cars, with a well-deserved reputation for fine quality and sleekness of design.

1934 DUESENBERG MODEL J SPEEDSTER

Many auto manufacturers were not able to survive the Great Depression era of economic collapse because luxury items like sports cars became the exclusive province of the rich and famous. Duesenberg was one of the prestigious auto makers to emerge from this time by catering to just such a market, offering meticulously hand-crafted, custom-designed bodies combined with a powerful eight-cylinder engine.

The company was founded by brothers Frederick and August Duesenberg in 1920. Duesenbergs were very successful on the racing circuit, winning the Indianapolis 500 and a number of European Grand Prix races. In 1926, the company was taken over by innovative automobile entrepreneur E. L. Cord. The premier version of the Duesenberg was the model "J" introduced in 1929. Built in a number of body styles—including coupe, roadster, and sedan— the model J was equipped with a powerful straight-eight engine capable of developing 265 hp. In 1933, a supercharger was added to the engine, boosting its power to an impressive 320 hp. So equipped, the Model "SJ" could reach 120 mph. Duesenberg ceased production in 1937, after a total production run of just 650 vehicles. Of this number, around 470 were the classic Model J's and SJ's. At around $17,000 each, these expensive and powerful automobiles became associated with the wealthy and elite members of American society, including politicians, industrial tycoons, and especially Hollywood movie stars. Clark Gable, Gary Cooper, and Mae West all had publicity photos shot while posing with their "Duesies."

1935 AUBURN MODEL 851 "BOATTAIL" SPEEDSTER

The Auburn Auto Company was another great name associated with sporty American automobiles of the 1930s. Shown above is their most famous vehicle, the Model 851 "Boattail" Speedster. So called for its gracefully tapered rear deck, the boattail was designed by famed automotive stylist, Gordon Buehrig. Introduced in 1928, the Speedster was powered by a supercharged straight-eight engine of 279 cubic-inches and 100 hp. Four stainless steel exhaust pipes exited through the side of the hood and down through the rear. From 1932 to 1934, Speedsters were also available with V-12 engines, producing 165 hp. Each vehicle was fitted with a plaque mounted on the dashboard certifying that it had been driven to 100 mph. These classic vehicles were created by the Auburn-Cord-Duesenberg Automobile Company of Auburn, Indiana, which finally ended production in 1937.

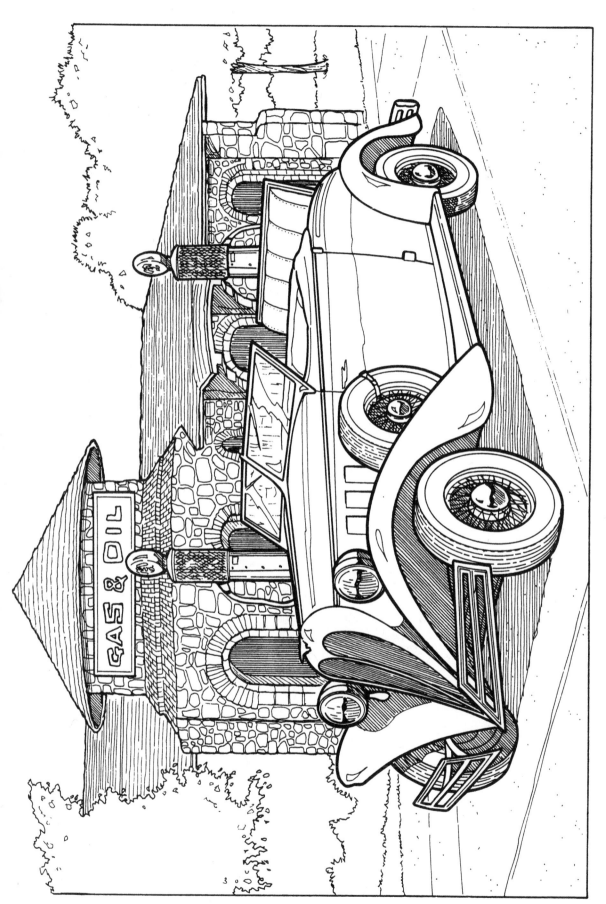

1935 BREWSTER CONVERTIBLE COUPE
was powered by a V-8 engine that produced 145 hp and could propel the vehicle to a top speed of 90 mph. Brewsters were built with custom-designed bodies mounted on Ford or Buick chassis (frames). They were manufactured in Springfield, Massachusetts from 1934 to 1936, and sold in the $3,000 to $3,500 range.

A unique-looking automobile of the 1930s was the limited production Brewster. Shown above is a 1935 Brewster Convertible Coupe, distinguished by its graceful heart-shaped grill-radiator, flowing fender lines, and very large headlights. It also features a classic "rumble seat" in the trunk area for carrying occasional passengers. This model of Brewster

GAS & OIL

7

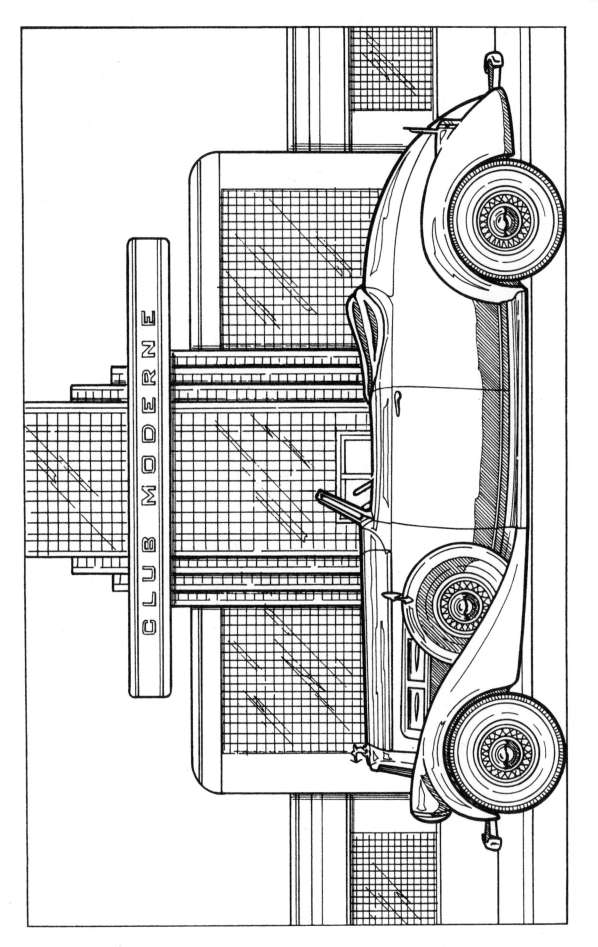

1935 PIERCE ARROW CONVERTIBLE ROADSTER

Despite the popular notion that most American cars came from Detroit, several auto makers were headquartered in New York State during this period. These included Cunningham Motors in Rochester, Franklin and Stutz on Long Island, and the Pierce Motor Car Company founded in Buffalo in 1901. By the 1930s, the Pierce "Arrow" had earned a reputation as a fast and luxurious sports car.

The convertible roadster shown above could be had with either a 385 cubic-inch straight-eight engine developing 140 hp, or a massive 462 cubic-inch V-12 that generated 175 hp. The Pierce Arrow came in a number of body styles, with each vehicle possessing a hand-crafted custom-made body. At a price of up to $10,000 each, the Pierce Arrow, like the Duesenberg, was available only to very affluent auto enthusiasts.

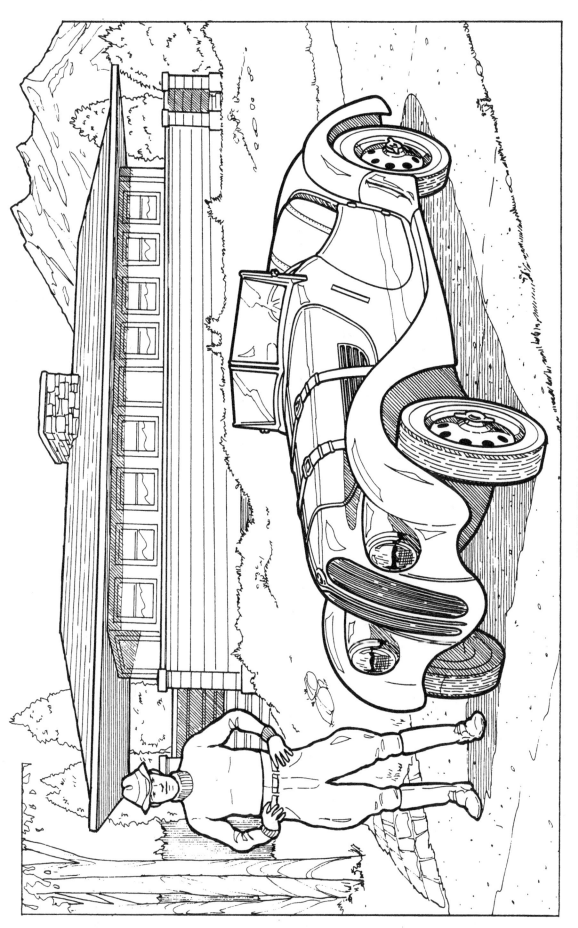

1936 BMW 328 ROADSTER

The German industrial firm of BMW began with the manufacture of aircraft engines just prior to World War I. By 1920 they were building a line of popular motorcycles, and in 1929 they began selling automobiles. BMW was heavily influenced by the auto racing technology of the day, and their sports cars reflected this interest. One of BMW's classic pre-World War II designs was the model 328 roadster shown above. With a streamlined body weighing only 1,930 pounds, the 328 was swift and agile through curves and around corners. It was powered by an advanced 120 cubic-inch six-cylinder engine fueled by triple carburetors. Putting out 80 hp to drive the lightweight body, the engine could propel the 328 to 95 mph. BMW would later become one of the premier automobile manufacturers of the modern era. Their sports sedans are world-renowned for their impressive power, exceptional handling, and outstanding quality.

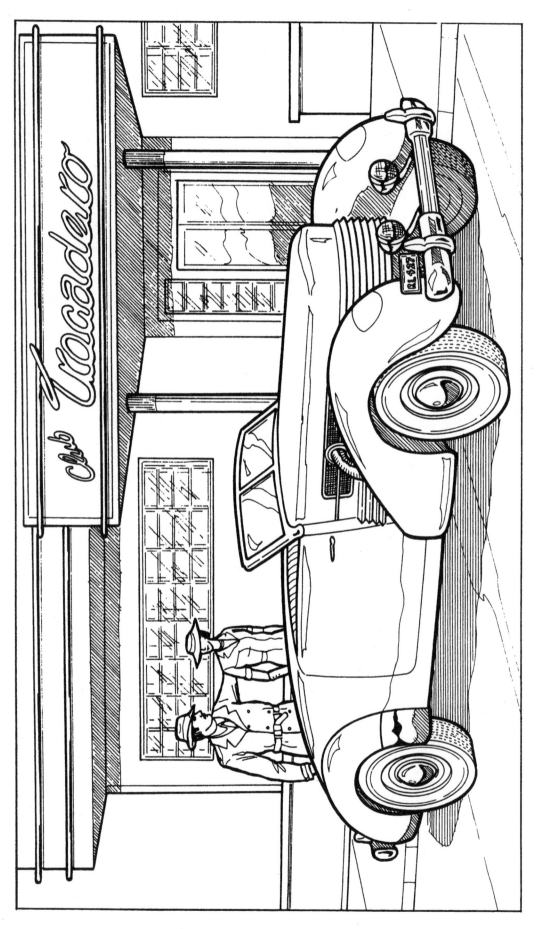

1937 CORD 812 SPORTSMANS CONVERTIBLE COUPE

One of the great innovators in the American auto industry was E. L. (Errat Lobban) Cord. Hired in 1924 by the Auburn Auto Company to boost flagging sales, Cord became a partner, re-energized the company, and introduced a series of classic American cars.

His first triumph was the Cord L-29, built from 1929 to 1932. Long, low, and fast, it sold very well. In 1935, Cord's most famous model—the 810—hit the streets. Designed by the prominent auto stylist Gordon Buehrig, the 810 quickly won over both the public and the motoring press. Incorporating innovative and futuristic features such as hidden pop-up headlights, front-wheel drive, and four-speed electric pre-selector transmission, the 810 turned heads whether in coupe, sedan, or roadster body styles. It was powered by a 288 cubic-inch V-8 engine that produced 115 hp, or a supercharged version that developed 190 hp. The distinctive "coffin-nosed" Cord 810 and its follow-up model the 812, were produced from 1935 to 1937. Today, these gems are defining examples of American streamline car design of the 1930s; and they are among the most expensive and sought-after vehicles in the classic car collectors' market.

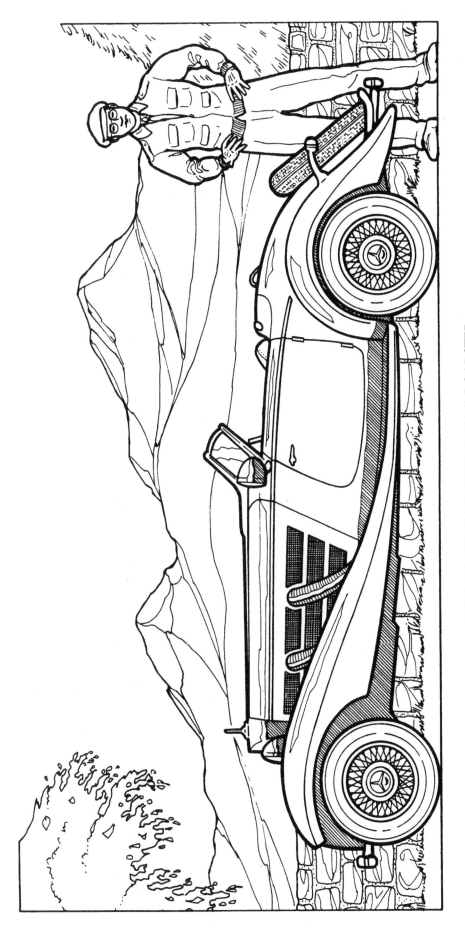

1938 MERCEDES-BENZ TYPE 500 K ROADSTER

Mercedes-Benz automobiles have always enjoyed a reputation for power, performance, and rock-solid quality. The company was founded in Germany by three pioneering giants of the early motor vehicle industry: Karl Benz, Wilhelm Maybach, and Gottlieb Daimler. Karl Benz is generally credited with being the "father" of the automobile with the invention of his first three-wheeled "motor carriage" in 1883. Wilhelm Maybach was among the first to mass-produce efficient and reliable internal-combustion engines for early motorized vehicles. And Gottlieb Daimler built the first motorcycle in 1885. The first "Mercedes" was built by Maybach and Daimler in 1900, and named after Mercedes Jellinek, the daughter of one of their financial backers. In 1926, they teamed up with Benz to form the Mercedes-Benz Company.

Throughout the first three decades of the 20th century, the company was very active in racing car manufacture for both Europe and the United States. Mercedes-Benz translated the technology gained from this experience into high-performance passenger sedans and sports cars. Shown above is one of their most well-designed pre-war models, the 1938 type 500 K Special Sports Roadster. Its engine was a super-charged straight-eight of 5,400 cc's. With 160 hp to drive the light-weight roadster body, the Type 500 K could reach 110 mph. It sold for a price of $10,780, a considerable amount of money in the late 1930s. To this day, Mercedes-Benz builds exceptional, high-performance luxury vehicles and sports cars.

11

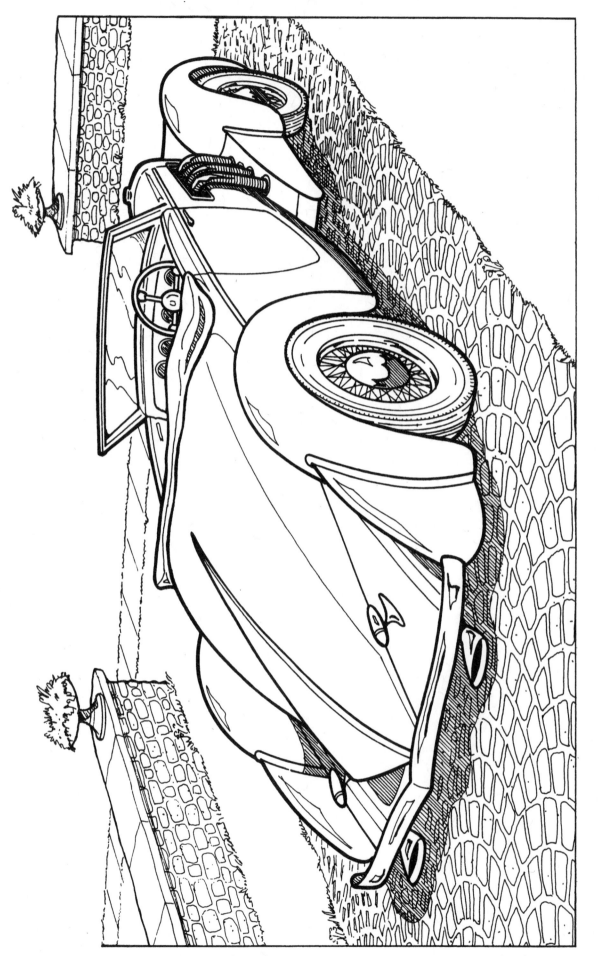

1938 DELAGE D8 ROADSTER

Louis Delage was one of the pioneers of the French auto industry, introducing his first vehicle in 1905. His cars soon gained a reputation for quality and style so that by the 1920s, Delage was firmly established as an innovative European auto maker. The Delage model D1 of 1927 was equipped with a powerful and advanced V-12 engine. The Delage shown above is a 1938 model D8 Roadster. It was powered by a straight-eight engine, developing an impressive 170 hp. The influence of American streamline design is obvious in the D8. Its gently curving fenders and trunk lid lead directly into aerodynamically-styled "fins," probably the first automotive application of this design device. Fins incorporated into automobile bodies would almost become a trademark of American cars of the 1950s and early 1960s.

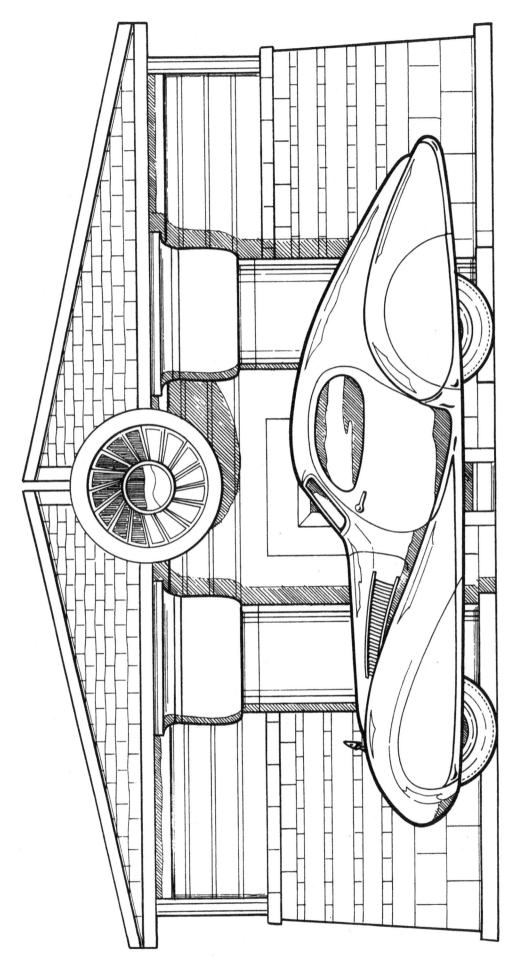

1939 TALBOT LAGO TYPE 150C SS COUPE

Another stylish French sports car of this period was the Talbot Lago Type 150C SS coupe. Nicknamed the "Aerodynamica" for its flowing and blended curves, the low-slung sportster looked fast even when parked. Created by Antoine Lago after acquiring the British Talbot Motors company, this unique vehicle was styled by the revered Italian design team of Joseph Figoni and Ovidio Falaschi. It was powered by a 4,000-cc six-cylinder engine generating 140 hp. With a top speed of 120 mph, the Talbot Lago Type 150C offered performance to match its racy appearance.

13

1939 BUGATTI TYPE 57 ROADSTER

Ettore Bugatti founded his automobile company in Molsheim, France in 1910. Like numerous other early car makers, many of Bugatti's vehicles were star competitors in motor car racing. With this background, he established a reputation for building fast and luxurious sports cars. One of Bugatti's classic designs was the Type 57, shown above in a 1939 roadster model. The Type 57 series was produced from 1934 until 1940, with a total of 670 vehicles in both coupe and convertible body styles. The Type 57 was equipped with a 3,300-cc eight-cylinder engine pumping out a healthy 200 hp.

The 1939 Type 57 was among the last of the great sports cars produced during this period. The onrushing tide of World War II soon swept away production facilities for these classic vehicles. By 1940, auto makers and other industrial plants in Europe and America were transformed into war materiel manufacturers, rolling out airplanes, tanks, and artillery instead of sleek, expensive sports cars. It was not until the early 1950s that auto makers were able to resume large-scale civilian auto production.

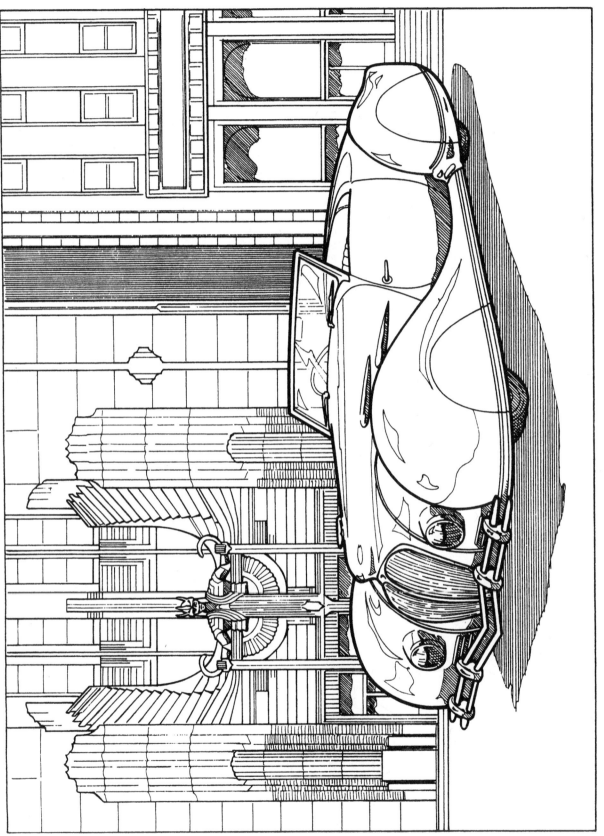

1947 DELAHAYE 135 CABRIOLET

The stylish 1947 French Delahaye 135, shown above, was more of a holdover from the 1939 models than an entirely new concept. It was intended to reinvigorate the French sports car market after the end of World War II. Its streamlined body featured metal "skirts" covering the front and rear wheels, presenting a smooth, unbroken line to the onlooker. Styled by Figoni and Falaschi, the sumptuous appearance of the Delahaye 135 would soon give way to the more modest designs of the early 1950s.

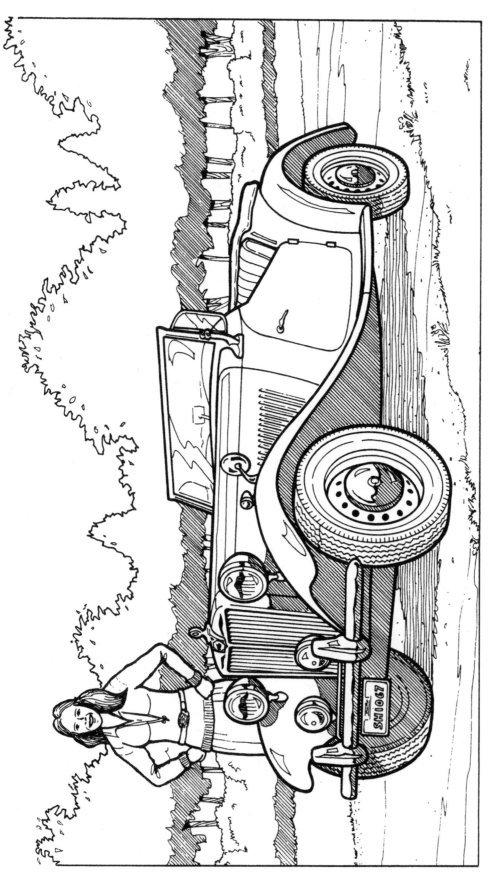

1950 MG TD ROADSTER

The grandfather of the modern post-war sports car was the low-slung, fast and lively, but hard-riding MG TD, pictured above. First introduced in England in 1946 as the MG TC with right-hand drive typical of British automobiles, it became very popular with the American servicemen still stationed in Europe. The model TC was built from 1946 to 1949, with a total production of over 10,000 vehicles. In 1950 MG Motors (MG stands for Morris Garages), perceiving the huge opportunity offered by the American market, brought out the slightly restyled MG TD featuring left-hand drive for export to the United States.

The MG TD was the epitome of the classic British two-seat open "roadster" sports car. Along with rivals Triumph and Jaguar, Great Britain had the lion's share of the world market for these kinds of cars during the 1950s and early 1960s. At around $2,000, the MG TD was inexpensive and fun to drive. With its 76 cubic-inch four-cylinder engine putting out only 54 hp, it was not very fast; but at a weight of just 1,930 pounds, the MG TD was quick and responsive through the curves. Between 1950 and 1953, MG built 29,664 model TD's, most of them for the American market. In 1953, a somewhat faster version—the MG TF with 76hp—was introduced, and manufactured until 1955. The TF was later superseded in 1955 by the all new, more advanced MGA roadster.

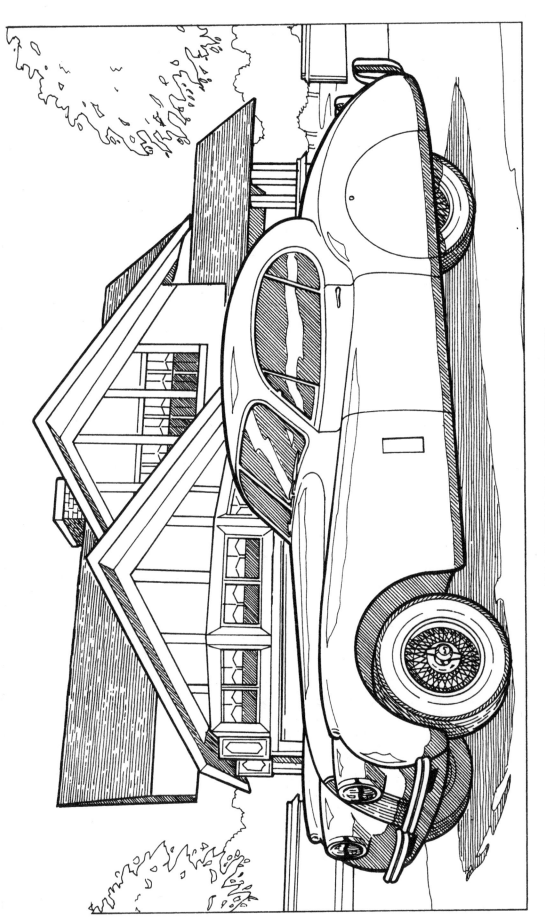

1951 JAGUAR XK 120 HARDTOP COUPE

Jaguar Motors re-emerged after World War II with the first in a line of fast and luxurious sports cars—the XK 120. Introduced in 1948, the XK 120 was initially available only as a convertible roadster. In 1951, Jaguar brought out the stylish hardtop coupe pictured above. The XK 120 was powered by the 3,400-cc straight-six engine fueled by twin carburetors. The engine's 160 hp could propel the 2,900-pound vehicle to a top speed of 125 mph. With its wood and leather-trimmed interior, superb handling qualities, and powerful engine, the XK 120 was the standard by which all other sports cars of this era were mea-sured. A total of 12,078 XK 120 models were built by Jaguar from 1948 to 1954.

In 1954, Jaguar introduced the XK 140, a more powerful model of the XK series. It was equipped with a 210-hp six-cylinder engine. From 1954 to 1957, Jaguar produced a total of 8,884 model XK 140's. The final version of this classic series of Jaguars was the XK 150, built from 1957 to 1960. It was the first to feature an automatic transmission in place of the four-speed manual gearbox. By 1960, Jaguar was ready to introduce its all-new sports car, the legendary model XK E.

1953 CHEVROLET CORVETTE

A milestone in the sports car world and in American auto manufacturing was introduced in 1953 by the Chevrolet division of the automotive giant General Motors. The innovative fiberglass-bodied Corvette hit the market in 1953 at a price of around $2,600. The first year just 300 vehicles were produced. In today's classic car market, one of those first 300 Corvettes is worth many times its original cost. With 1950's "jet-age" styling by the GM genius of auto design Harley Earl, the Corvette's smooth aerodynamic shape even featured tiny fins atop the tail-light extensions.

In 1953–54, Corvettes were only available with Chevrolet's reliable "blue-flame" six-cylinder engine. With triple carburetors and dual exhausts, the engine developed 150 hp. With the introduction of a V-8 engine in 1955, the Corvette became a serious contender for the sports car market. Its first V-8 was a 265 cubic-inch engine developing 195 hp. This gave the Corvette an impressive 0 to 60 mph speed of just 8.5 seconds. In 1956, the engine was modified to produce 240 hp, lowering the 0 to 60 time to 7.5 seconds. By 1957, Chevy's revered "283" V-8 engine was available in Corvettes. With Rochester fuel-injection, the 283 V-8 pumped out 270 hp, making the 3,100-pound car blindingly fast. Its 0–60 time fell to only 5.7 seconds and gave the Corvette a top speed of 132 mph. Chevrolet had created an instant legend in the sports car field. And succeeding generations of the Corvette would just get better and better.

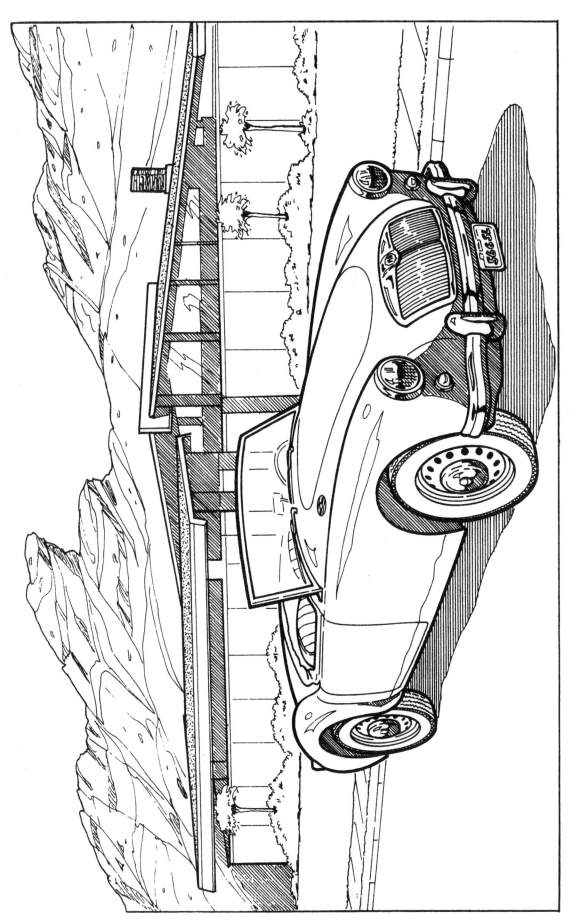

1955 MGA ROADSTER

While Jaguar was dominating the high end of the sports car price spectrum, the MG's were holding their own in the less expensive portion of the market. Having sold over 49,000 of the earlier models of TC's, TD's, and TF's, MG Motors introduced their new and completely restyled MGA in 1955. Selling initially for around $3,000, this sleek-looking model became the most popular MG ever built, with a total of 101,000 produced from 1955 to 1962.

The MGA featured a four-cylinder engine of 1,489 cc's and 72 hp in its first few years of manufacture. The engine size and power were gradually increased during the MGA's production run, first to 1,588 cc's and 80 hp, then to 1,622 cc's and 85 hp. The final version featured a twin-cam 1,622-cc engine pumping out 108 hp. For a 2,200-pound vehicle, that amount of horsepower made for a very quick sports car. The MGA ceased production in 1962, making way for the new model MGB.

1957 FORD THUNDERBIRD

The Ford Motor Company battled its rival Chevrolet for the lead in American auto sales during the '50s and '60s. The Thunderbird, introduced in 1955, was Ford's answer to the Chevy Corvette. The T-bird, as it was also known, was a two-seat sports car with typical '50s styling—lots of chrome, wide whitewall tires, and flashy tail fins. It was powered by a 292 cubic-inch V-8 engine, developing 200 hp. With a massive four-barrel carburetor and dual exhausts exiting through the rear bumper, the Thunderbird could reach 60 mph in just 8 seconds. The two-seat version was sold as a convertible and included a removable fiberglass hardtop.

In 1955, the T-bird's first year of production, Ford sold a total of 16,155 vehicles. This represented a staggering 24-to-1 sales ratio over the Corvette. Ford changed the concept of the Thunderbird for the 1958 model year, redesigning it as a four-seat "sport luxury vehicle" intended to appeal to a broader market. In this configuration, the T-bird continued to thrive until 1997, when production ceased. Ford has announced its intention to revive the Thunderbird in its original two-seat form sometime after the year 2000.

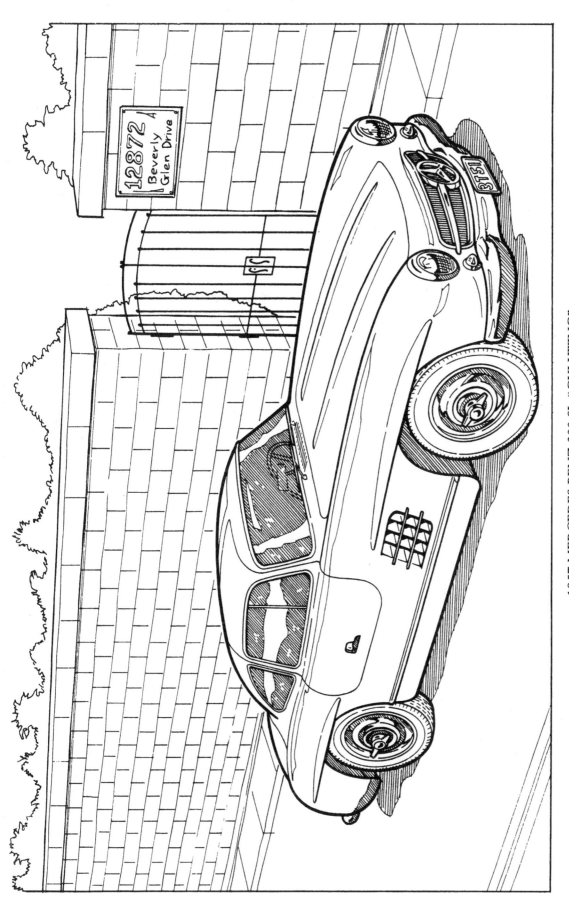

1957 MERCEDES-BENZ 300 SL "GULLWING"

Like the trio of venerated British sports cars—the Jaguar, MG, and Triumph— Germany also produced three formidable contributions to the high-performance sports car market. Mercedes-Benz, BMW, and Porsche are all highly esteemed for their technologically advanced and impeccably styled automobiles. A true classic was created by Mercedes-Benz with the introduction of the "gull-wing" 300 SL coupe in 1954. Its most striking feature, of course, are the unique doors that open upward from hinges along the roof's centerline. The 300 SL was an immediate hit with both the public and the motoring press.

The 300 SL's elegantly designed body was fabricated from aluminum and steel, and weighed just 2,710 pounds. It was powered by a 3,000-cc in-line six-cylinder engine. This fuel-injected powerplant pumped out an impressive 240 hp, giving the 300 SL a speedy 0–60 time of just 7.5 seconds, and a top speed of 140 mph. Mercedes-Benz produced only 1,400 of these treasured 300 SL gullwing coupes from 1954 to 1957. A roadster model was introduced in 1957 and built until 1963.

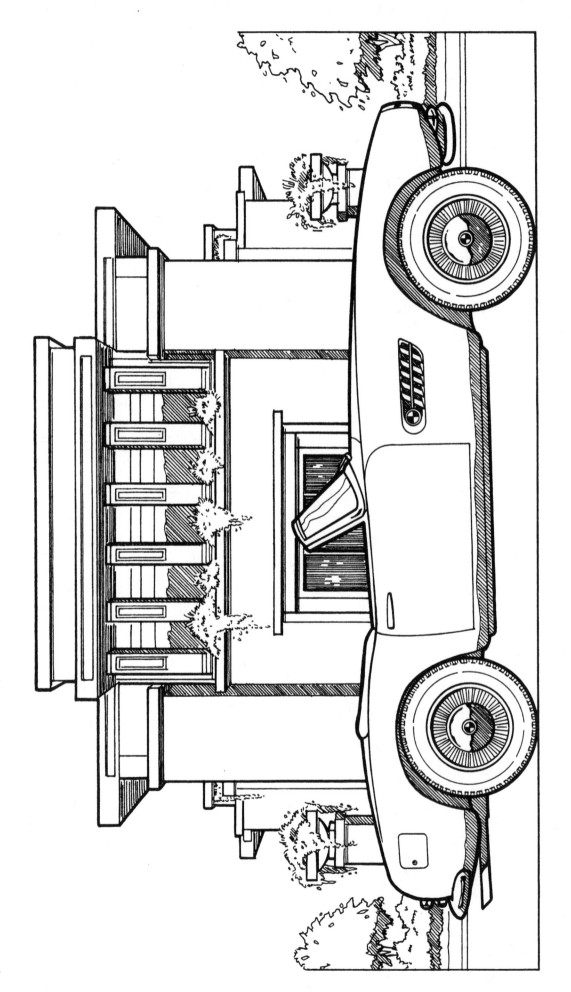

1958 BMW 507 ROADSTER

BMW introduced their model 507, a handsome, aluminum-bodied two-seat roadster in 1956. Intended to compete with Mercedes-Benz and Porsche convertibles, the 507 had speed and verve. It featured a lightweight all-aluminum V-8 engine of 3,168 cc's that produced 150 hp. The 507 could accelerate to 60 mph in 8.5 seconds and hit 135 mph. From 1956 to 1959, BMW built just 252 of these simple but elegant sports roadsters.

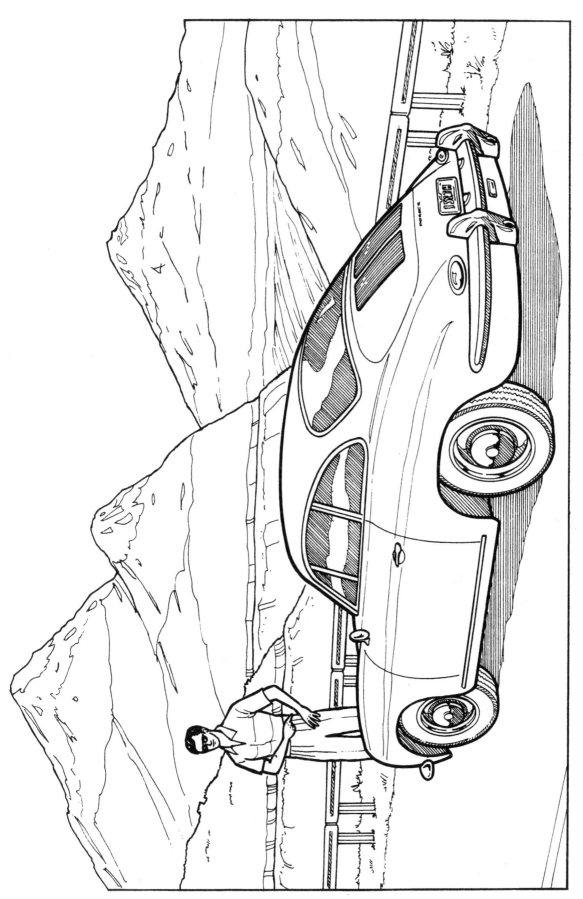

1959 PORSCHE 356 B

The third member of the triad of great German sports cars of the '50s was the Porsche 356. It was introduced in 1951 with a rear-mounted, 1,300-cc horizontally-opposed four-cylinder engine. Through the decade of the '50s, the engine size was gradually increased to 1,582 cc's by the time of the emergence of the 1959 model 356 B, shown above. With dual carburetors and dual exhausts, the engine produced 105 hp. It gave the 1,970-pound vehicle a 0–60 mph time of 10.5 seconds and a top speed of 105 mph. A total of 30,963 Porsche 356 coupes and roadsters were sold from 1951 to their final year of production in 1965. In that year, the 356 was replaced by the most enduring line of Porsche sports cars ever produced—the 911 series.

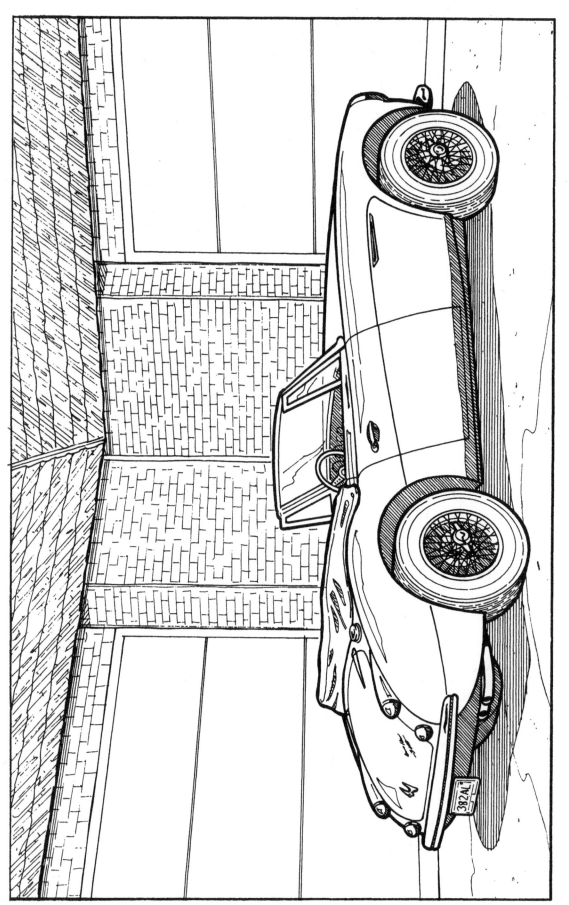

1960 AUSTIN HEALEY 3000

Another fine example of the preeminent British sports roadster is illustrated above. It is a 1960 Austin Healey model 3000. These two-seat convertibles were positioned in the sports car market between the less expensive MG's and the costlier Jaguars. They began production in 1953 as the series 100. These first Austin Healeys were powered by a 2,600-cc four-cylinder engine developing 124 hp. The model designation 100 denoted a top speed of 100 mph. In 1956, a six-cylinder engine producing 132 hp was introduced. By 1959, the engine size had increased to 3,000-cc and 150 hp. Equipped with this engine, the Austin Healey could reach 60 mph in 9.5 seconds and hit a top speed of 120 mph. This more powerful version was designated the Austin Healey 3000. Production of these models continued until 1968. A total of 72,022 four- and six-cylinder Austin Healeys were built from 1953 to 1968. The majority of these fast and stylish British roadsters were exported to the U.S. market.

1962 ASTON MARTIN DB4

A number of expensive sports-luxury automobiles with lower production volumes have been created by various European and American car makers. Shown above is the prestigious Aston Martin DB4 hardtop coupe. Featuring a high-powered six-cylinder engine fueled by triple carburetors and generating a hefty 240 hp, the DB4 had a top speed of 140 mph. The DB4 was produced from 1958 to 1963. Its successor, the DB5 coupe, gained fame and popularity as the machine gun and radar-equipped vehicle driven by James Bond in the 1964 film, "Goldfinger." The last of this series was the DB6, which was made until 1970. A limited production run of only 3,876 DB series cars from 1958 to 1970 has guaranteed their value in today's classic car collectors' market.

1962 MGB ROADSTER

The replacement for the immensely popular MGA sports roadster was introduced in the 1962 model year. This was the MGB convertible depicted above. It too enjoyed great popularity and sales success. From its initial year of manufacture in 1962 until 1980—its final year of production—MG Motors sold a huge volume of 512,243 MGB's.

The MGB was equipped with a peppy 1,798-cc four-cylinder engine, developing 95 hp. With its lightweight roadster body of just 2,030 pounds, the MGB could reach 105 mph and had a 0–60 mph time of 11.5 seconds. By 1965, a fastback hardtop coupe had been introduced to complement the roadster. Equally well received, a total of 125,322 of these stylish coupes were built.

1966 AC COBRA

Many sports car enthusiasts consider the AC Cobra pictured above to be the ultimate incarnation of the British two-seat open roadster. However, it is actually a mixture of British and American technologies. The Cobra is powered by either of two high performance V-8 engines made by the Ford Motor Company. When it was introduced in 1962 by AC Motors of Great Britain, it was equipped with a 289 cubic-inch Ford V-8 tuned to deliver 300 hp. Built and sold in partnership with American racing driver and automotive engineer, Carroll Shelby, the Cobra was all brute power in a 2,000-pound aluminum body.

In 1965, Shelby created the ultimate street racer when he mated the Cobra body with Ford's most powerful engine, the 427 cubic-inch V-8. With two four-barrel carburetors and side-exiting dual exhausts, the 427 Cobra engine generated a tremendous 425 hp. With this combination of power and light weight, the 427 Cobra had a staggering 0-60 mph time of just 4.2 seconds and could reach a top speed of 165 mph. The AC Shelby 427 Cobra was produced from 1965 to 1968 with a very low production volume of only 316 vehicles. Needless to say, in today's car collectors' market they are very scarce and highly prized.

1967 ALFA ROMEO SPIDER

Italy has produced many great names in the sports car world including Ferrari, Maserati, Lamborghini, Fiat, and Alfa Romeo. One of the most popular and best-selling Italian sports cars has been the Alfa Romeo Spider shown above. Introduced in 1966, its sleek stylish body was created by the Italian design studio of Pininfarina. The Spider was powered by a dual-overhead cam 1,600-cc four-cylinder aluminum engine. With its high-performance engine rated at 125 hp, the Spider had a 0–60 time of 10.5 seconds and could achieve 115 mph. In 1969, the Spider received a larger 2,000-cc engine. With this 135 hp motor, the Spider's 0–60 mph time dropped to a speedy 9.5 seconds. The Alfa Romeo Spider gained enormous publicity, followed by huge demand, when it was prominently featured in the 1967 hit movie, "The Graduate." The Spider continued in production with revised and upgraded versions until 1993.

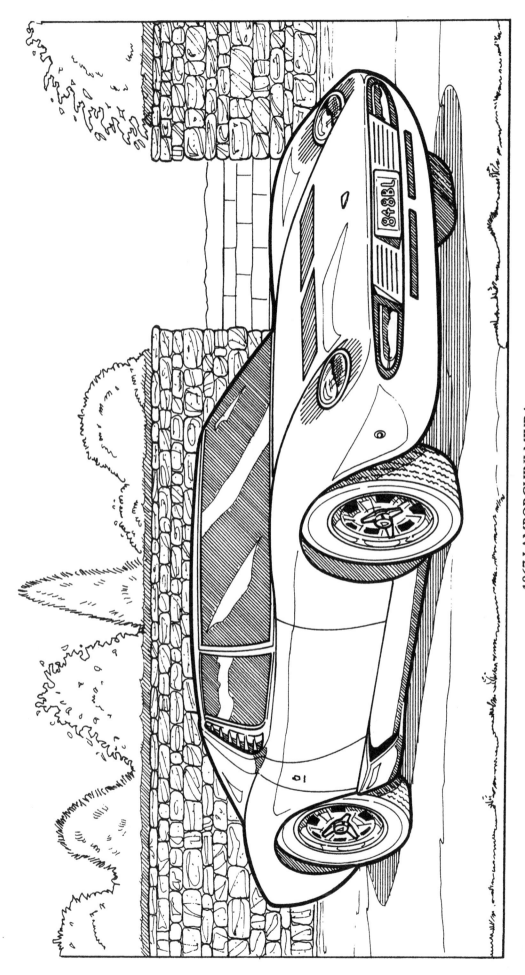

1967 LAMBORGHINI MIURA

The Lamborghini Miura was one of the first in a series of "super sports cars" that were created in the 1960s by several European car makers. These expensive and exotically designed vehicles were the ultimate in speed, handling, and luxury. They were produced in small numbers by companies such as Lamborghini, Ferrari, Maserati, Lotus, Aston Martin, Porsche, and BMW for the sports car buyer for whom price was no object.

The Miura—whose name derived from a breed of Spanish fighting bull—first appeared in 1966, and was immediately acclaimed for its speed and design. It was powered by a sophisticated V-12 engine mounted sideways and located midway between the front and rear of the car. With this near-perfect front to back weight balance, the Miura could shoot through curves and around corners at blazing speeds. For its first two years of production, the V-12 engine was rated at 350 hp. In 1968, it was increased to 370 hp, and by 1972—the last year the Miura was built—it rose to 385 hp. In that most powerful version, the vehicle had a top speed of 175 mph, and a 0–60 mph time of 5.5 seconds. From 1966 to 1972, Lamborghini produced just 800 of these powerful and stylish Miuras.

1967 FORD MUSTANG SHELBY COBRA GT-500

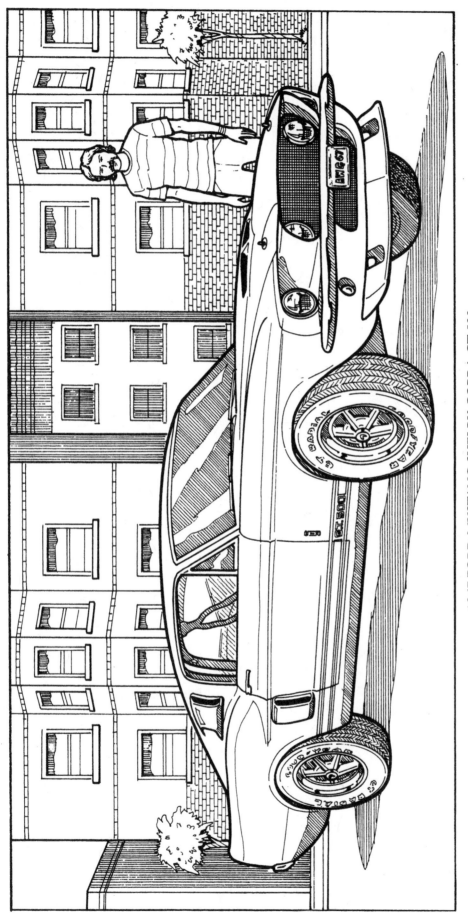

While the Europeans were producing small quantities of fast and luxurious "super cars," American car makers introduced a new breed of sporty automobile. The "Pony" car was introduced in 1964, and nicknamed after the first one of this type—the Ford Mustang. By 1966, all of the U.S. auto companies had created their own versions designed to meet the wildly enthusiastic public response to these cars. The Chevy Camaro, Pontiac Firebird, Plymouth Barracuda, and Dodge Challenger were produced in large numbers and enjoyed great popularity.

While these four-seat high-performance vehicles were not true sports cars in all their elements, they shared two features typical of American sports cars: a large and powerful V-8 engine in a lightweight body. Because the competition in this market became very keen, specialty models of the Pony cars were developed. The most famous of

these were the Ford Shelby Mustang Cobra GT-350 and GT-500, developed by Ford and auto engineer Carroll Shelby. The first Shelby Mustang was introduced in 1965—the model GT-350. It was powered by a race-tuned Ford 289 cubic-inch V-8 pumping out a beefy 270 hp. In 1967, Ford brought out the GT-350's big brother, the GT-500. Available in a stylish fastback coupe, the Shelby Cobra GT-500 was equipped with Ford's largest engine, the 428 cubic-inch "Police Interceptor" V-8, fueled by two four-barrel carburetors and developing a massive 360 hp.

In this configuration, the GT-500 had a 0–60 mph time of 6 seconds and a top end of 135 mph. Loaded with racing features such as aircraft-style shoulder-harness seatbelts, air dams and spoilers, hood and body side air scoops, and locking hood pins, the GT-500 was the ultimate American car of its era.

1969 DATSUN 240 Z

European sports car and motorcycle manufacturers dominated the world market during the first half of the 20th century. By the 1960s, Japan began to challenge that lead. In 1969, two Japanese companies brought out revolutionary vehicles that signaled the end of the long reign of the European manufacturers. In that year Honda Motors introduced their model CB750 to the motorcycle world. It was fast, reliable, stylish, and affordable, and opened up the American market to the Japanese motorcycle invasion. That same year, Datsun Motors—now called Nissan—introduced their sports car, the 240 Z, to the U.S. market.

The Datsun 240 Z had an attractive combination of power, stylish good looks, a reputation for quality, and a relatively low price tag of $3,500. It came equipped with a robust six-cylinder engine that delivered 160 hp. In the 2,250-pound vehicle, that powerplant could speed the 240 Z to 60 mph in 8 seconds and reach 125 mph. The 240 Z enjoyed great popularity and sales success. From 1969 to 1973, Datsun sold over 150,000 240 Z models. In 1973, Datsun introduced a more powerful version called the 260 Z. This was produced until 1978, when it was supplanted by the even faster 280 ZX. The final version of the 240 Z was the extremely powerful 300 ZX Turbo brought out in 1990.

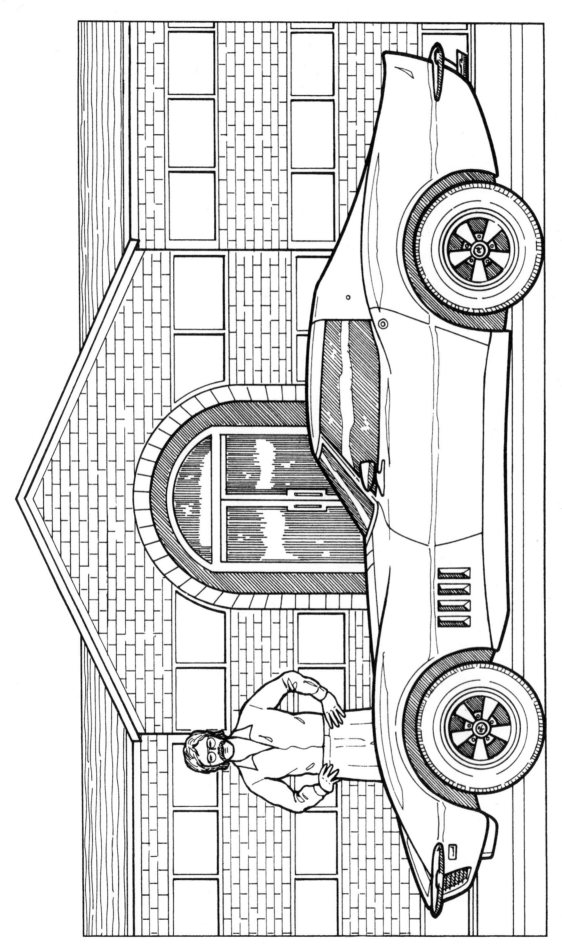

1970 CHEVROLET CORVETTE STINGRAY

In 1968, Chevrolet brought out an all-new model of the Corvette. Renamed the "Stingray" (one word), it was restyled by Bill Mitchell with muscular bulges, sweeping curves, and a shark-like pointed nose. This fourth generation body design was well-received by sports car fans—with Stingray sales of over 500,000 from its introduction in 1968 until it was once again restyled in 1978.

Corvette engine power reached its peak during the ten-year era of the Stingray. A larger 350 cubic-inch V-8 replaced the venerable "327" as the standard powerplant. The 350 engine was available in several horsepower levels ranging from the lowest at 180 hp, to the race-tuned LT-1 engine with 370 hp. The ultimate Corvette engine options were the big-block "454" cubic-inch V-8 producing 400 hp, and the legendary triple-carburetor "427" cubic-incher, pumping out a massive 435 hp. Equipped with this engine, the Stingray could reach a top speed of 160 mph and had a 0–60 mph time of just 5.3 seconds.

1971 JAGUAR XK E 2+2 V-12 COUPE

The successor to Jaguar Motors XK 100 series of sports cars of the 1950s was the XK E-type, introduced in 1961. With its simple and elegant body style, the E-type became an instant classic in both Europe and the U.S. Powered initially by a strong 3,781-cc six-cylinder engine producing 265 hp, the E-Jag was fast, nimble, and luxurious. An impressive 75,520 E-type Jaguars were sold during its production run from 1961 to 1975. The E-Jag was available in convertible roadster, coupe, and 2+2 fastback coupe body styles. For the 1971 model year, a technically advanced and powerful V-12 engine was added as an option. Producing close to 300 hp, this quadruple-carbureted powerplant could propel the E-Jag to a top speed of 145 mph. The E-type Jaguar stands as one of the most coveted and enduring sports cars ever created.

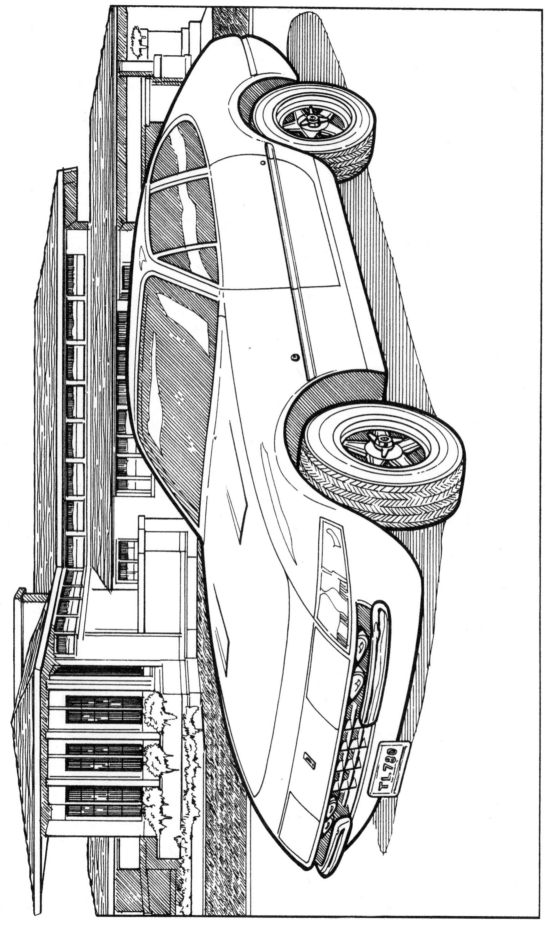

1971 FERRARI 365 GTB/4 DAYTONA

Ferrari's answer to the challenge of the exotic mid-engined Lamborghini Miura was their equally stunning model, the 365 GTB/4 Daytona, brought onto the market in 1968. The Daytona was widely admired both for its design and stunning performance. It featured a 4,390-cc V-12 engine fueled by no less than six carburetors. Generating 375 hp, the V-12 engine could push the Daytona to a blinding top speed of 175 mph, and gave it a 0-60 mph time of only 5.6 seconds. During the Daytona's years of production from 1968 to 1973, the Ferrari sold 1,274 of these high-performance vehicles. The rivalry between Ferrari and Lamborghini for fastest "super sports car" would continue to rage well into the 1990s.

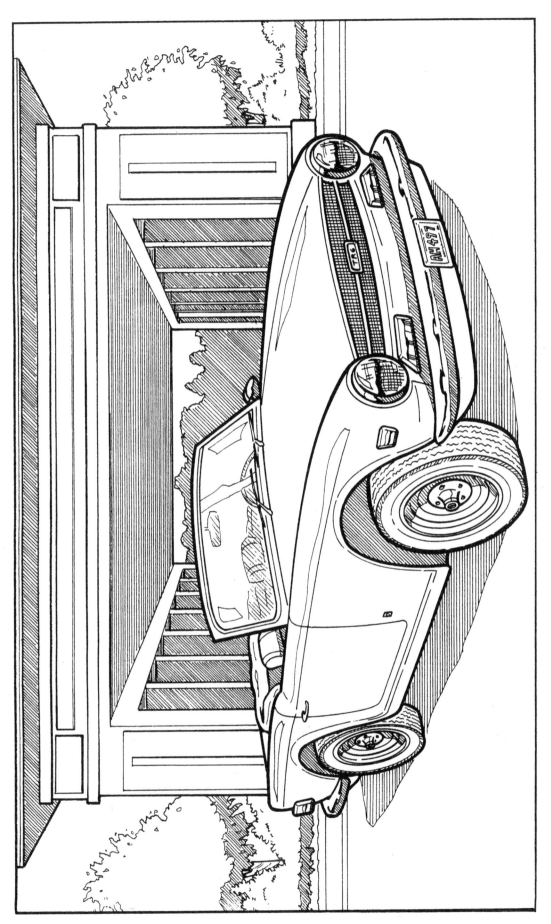

1973 TRIUMPH TR6 ROADSTER

At the other end of the price and performance spectrum from Ferrari and Lamborghini were the more affordable sports cars offered by MG and Triumph. A classic series of British two-seat roadsters, the Triumph TR models date back to the original TR2 built from 1953 to 1955. They were powered by progressively more powerful four-cylinder engines in the TR3 (1958–61), and the TR4 (1965–67). The TR5 of 1967 through 1969 brought a more powerful six-cylinder engine into the series line-up. These lively little sports cars were enthusiastically embraced by the American market during their years of production.

For the 1969 model year, Triumph released a newly restyled roadster, the TR6. This smart-looking convertible was equipped with a 2,500-cc six-cylinder engine, developing 150 hp. The 1973 model pictured above could reach 60 mph in 8.2 seconds and could top out at 119 mph. In 1976, Triumph introduced the totally revamped TR7 model in both coupe and roadster styles. Its unusual wedge-shaped body met with mixed reviews by both the public and the motoring press, and production ended after just two years.

1973 FIAT 124 SPORT SPIDER

A worthy competitor to Triumph and MG in the lower priced sports car market was the Fiat 124 Sport Spider, depicted above. Introduced into the U.S. market in 1968, the 124 Spider enjoyed a well-deserved reputation for its swift and sprightly road handling qualities. With crisp styling by the celebrated design group Pininfarina, the 124 was available in the open roadster model or a four-seat coupe version. Power was provided by a high-performance four-cylinder, twin overhead cam engine of 1,587-cc and 92 hp. So armed, the 124 Spider had a 0–60 mph time of 12.5 seconds. However, raw speed was never the Spider's forte. Instead, the Spider provided thrills and excitement as it whipped expertly around curves and corners at speeds that would have sent more ordinary cars spinning onto two wheels. The 124 Sport Spider was sold from 1968 to 1984. Fiat pulled out of the U.S. market that year because of poor sales and emission control standards they could not meet.

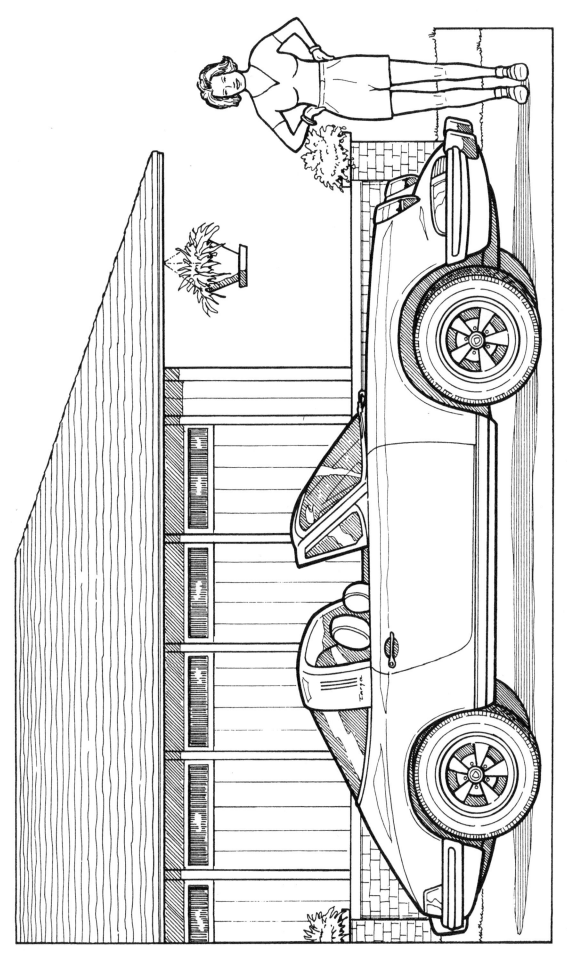

1975 PORSCHE 911 TARGA

Many sports car fans would consider the Porsche 911 series to be the best high-performance sporting automobiles ever marketed. Introduced in 1964 to replace the 356 series of models, the 911 is still being produced in several versions. The 911 was initially powered by a rear-mounted, 2,000-cc six-cylinder engine developing 130 hp. The horizontally-opposed "boxer" engine gradually increased in size and power over the years. By 1967, the engine had grown to 2,200 cc's and 160 hp. In 1973, the 911 Carrera RS was introduced with a 2,700-cc engine generating 210 hp. Between 1978 and 1990, the engine grew to 3,000 cc's, 3,200 cc's, and finally to 3,600 cc's. With that powerplant, the 250 hp 911 had a top speed of 150 mph and a 0–60 time of 5.6 seconds. Shown above is a 1975 911 "Targa" with a removable center hardtop.

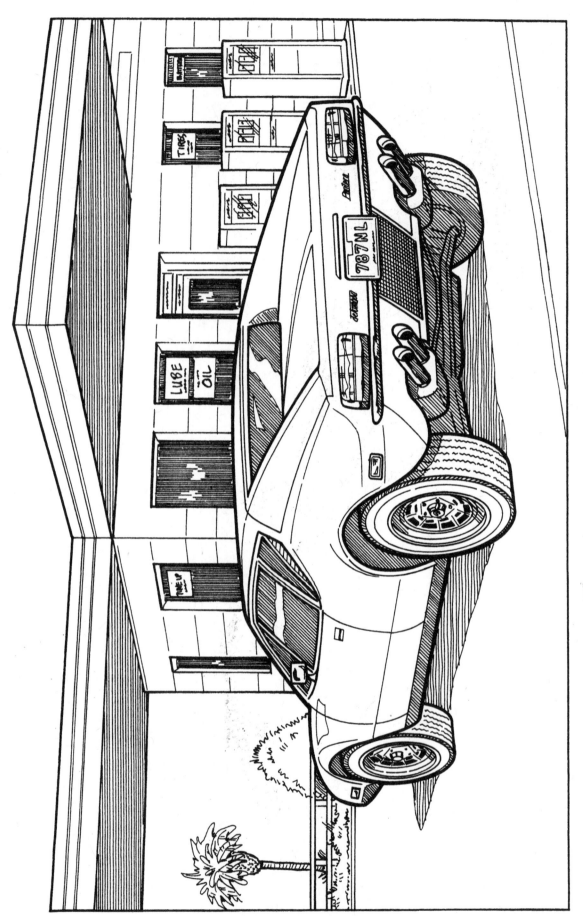

1975 DETOMASO PANTERA

Pictured above is a powerful and sleek hybrid of European design and American engine power. The DeTomaso Pantera (Panther) was a joint project between Ford and the small-volume Italian car maker DeTomaso Automobili. It was powered by a mid-engine 351 cubic-inch Ford V-8 generating 300 hp. With its lightweight body being driven by that amount of horsepower, the Pantera could reach 60 mph in 5.5 seconds and had a top speed of 160 mph. The Pantera was built between 1971 and 1973 for sale in the U.S. In 1974, the DeTomaso company was bought by Italian sports car maker Maserati, who continued production of an upgraded version of the Pantera exclusively for European sales until 1990.